Chain Your Trauma

Train Your Change

Allison M. Everly

Copyright © 2021 Allison M. Everly
All rights reserved.

The content contained within this book may not be reproduced, duplicated or transmitted without direct written permission from the author or the publisher.
Under no circumstances will any blame or legal responsibility be held against the publisher, or author, for any damages, reparation, or monetary loss due to the information contained within this book, either directly or indirectly.

Legal Notice:
This book is copyright protected. It is only for personal use. You cannot amend, distribute, sell, use, quote or paraphrase any part, or the content within this book, without the consent of the author or publisher.

Disclaimer Notice:
Please note the information contained within this document is for educational and entertainment purposes only. All effort has been executed to present accurate, up to date, reliable, complete information. No warranties of any kind are declared or implied. Readers acknowledge that the author is not engaged in the rendering of legal, financial, medical or professional advice. The content within this book has been derived from various sources. Please consult a licensed professional before attempting any techniques outlined in this book.
By reading this document, the reader agrees that under no circumstances is the author responsible for any losses, direct or indirect, that are incurred as a result of the use of the information contained within this document, including, but not limited to, errors, omissions, or inaccuracies.

ISBN: 9798529558287

To all the wounded angels who want to take a step towards overcoming their past obstacles and to begin truly living with a free and unchained heart. ♡

TABLE OF CONTENTS

Introduction 3

Chapter 1: 8

   Traumatic Stress from Childhood 10

   The Signs and Symptoms of PTSD 11

      The Connection Between PTSD and Self-Isolation 12

      The Connection Between PTSD and Dissociation 14

      The Connection Between PTSD and Relationships 15

   The Stages of Healing 19

Chapter 2: 21

   Step 1: Re-establish Bodily Safety 23

   Step 2: Re-establish Physical Safety 26

   Step 3: Re-establish Emotional Stability 30

Chapter 3: 35

   Making Peace With Your Inner Child 39

   The Energetic Nature of Trauma 43

      The EmotionAid Technique to Release Trauma from the Body 46

Chapter 4: 49

   Being Comfortable in Your Own Skin 51

   Building Trust in Relationships Post-Trauma 54

   Setting Meaningful Personal and Professional Goals 56

Chapter 5: 59

   Self-Awareness Leads to Happiness 60

- **Resilience in the Face of Adversity** 62
- Chapter 6: 65
  - Acceptance and Commitment Therapy 65
  - Mindfulness Meditation 67
- **A Letter to My Special Reader** 70
- Conclusion 72

ACKNOWLEDGMENTS

I would like to first and foremost thank my closest friend and companion for her continuous support in all that I've achieved and for the completion of this book. I would have never thought to write about trauma if it were not for the friendship between me and her. Never have I learned more about mental health conditions than I did with her – a wise, intelligent, and passionate young psychologist. She opened my eyes and heart to a separate world of understanding and empathy in these causes. Also, much thanks to my brother that made publishing this book possible, helped me through the process and supported me all the way.

INTRODUCTION

Have you watched the six o'clock news recently? What do you see? How many times does your heart stop beating for a few seconds due to the sheer shock of some of the horrors we hear about? I'm someone who loves being informed about what's happening around the world, however, I've had to restrict the number of times I turn on the TV or scroll through my social media feeds. The content we find on news reports, online articles, and social media posts are gradually becoming more and more cynical. It almost seems like everybody, everywhere, is having a bad day, month, or year!

I've asked myself many times where this dark and negative energy comes from. Who opened the gates of hell and forgot to close them? Upon further digging, I realized that the negative energy comes from all of us. Yes, we're responsible for pessimism that's in the air. It may not be our intention to infect those around us with our own fears, doubts, anxieties, or misery, but since energies are contagious, we can't help but spread it.

Going even deeper, I wanted to find out what causes people to adopt an inherently negative or pessimistic view on life. I found that people's outward behaviors and actions are a result of their inward beliefs, thoughts, and emotions. In other words, your behavior says a lot about what you think about yourself, how you feel about others, and how you perceive the world.

This made a lot of sense to me. It put the saying "It's not you, it's me" in perspective and made me realize that most of the chaos we see on the news or read about on our social media pages begins internally. When we're not at peace with ourselves and our own life's stories, we cannot find peace in our relationships with others, or feel safe in the world.

Before I could let this thought process go, I had one more question I needed answered. I wanted to know what causes internal chaos. What makes us feel broken inside, become suspicious of people, or emotionally detached in our relationships? A quote by the writer Laurell K. Hamilton guided me toward the answer. The quote reads, "There are wounds that never show on the body that are deeper and more hurtful than anything that bleeds."

The word "trauma" is translated as "wound" in Greek. This may be a physical or psychic wound that carries a painful shockwave when experienced in the body. Physical wounds are easily treatable because they are seen, but emotional wounds or emotional trauma can be hidden under false disguises, or buried deep in our innermost being so that it's barely detectable.

Back in college, I had a friend named Macy. We met in one of our classes and naturally gravitated toward each other. She was kind and soft-spoken, and we seemed to have a lot in common. Macy wasn't as social as I was, but we somehow found a way to make our friendship work. We would frequently binge-watch series together and spend hours talking about them afterward (she was the only person who understood my love for the sitcom Friends). When I couldn't make time to see her, we would keep each other in the loop, through text, but I'd notice in her subtle tone that she'd be bothered that I wasn't spending time with her. Deep down, I wished she was out and about with me, enjoying what the student nightlife had to offer.

It took me a while to realize Macy battled with a low self-esteem. Her behavior made a lot more sense and I immediately felt sympathy for her. From the little she told me about her life, I could tell she was going through an emotional storm . I started noticing when we would start talking, she would always speak negatively about herself. She would judge herself harshly and find ways of watering down her achievements. Having battled with a low self-esteem, I would reassure her that these self-limiting beliefs are not true. They had no factual evidence to validate them. Macy listened to me and appreciated my advice; she said it was the most anyone had ever cared for her.

Macy's negative self-esteem was due to growing up in a broken home. As a kid, she witnessed the dysfunctional relationship between her parents and grew up with difficulties forming healthy relationships with other people. Her parents were either overly affectionate with one another or calling each other names and threatening to leave. Their dysfunctional relationship leaked over into how they raised her. Macy's parents were always hot and cold; on some occasions they would praise her for doing well at school, and other times they would remind her of her inadequacies. Needless to say, Macy grew up with a lot of questions about who she was and where she fit in in life.

My friendship with Macy taught me the importance of healing from childhood wounds. The truth is that childhood wounds don't show up until later in life - when you're in college, just got a job, or finally met the love of your life. These wounds express themselves through self-destructive behaviors, beliefs, or impulses and cause you to relive the darkest moments of your past. In order to heal from trauma, you must chain it. Chaining it doesn't mean pretending the trauma doesn't exist or that it doesn't affect you, but it means actually confronting it, feeling it, and letting it stay in the past where it belongs.

After college, I had the privilege of interning at a local marketing agency. The agency was small, about 10 people in total, and we worked in what looked like an abandoned industrial warehouse. It probably sounds dangerous, but it gave me hipster vibes, which was right up my alley! The first day at work, I was greeted by a guy named Michael (or Mikey), and he became my office mentor. He showed me how all the design software worked, how to speak to clients, and how to make coffee for the whole office (I became the tea lady).

After work, Mikey and I would go out for a quick drink. He was only two years older than me, so we had a lot of things in common. He was a very open person and in between our conversations, he'd tell me stories about his childhood. One time, he told me a story of how his family was homeless when they immigrated from Mexico to the U.S. His father was promised a job at a manufacturing company, but to their dismay, the employer didn't provide any accommodation. They didn't know anybody living here who could take them in, so they lived on the streets of Houston for several months. None of them knew a word of English, nor did they understand how to fit into the American culture, but through adapting to what they saw and heard, they eventually felt comfortable with life in America.

When I heard this story, I found it very difficult to hold back my tears. We all have heard stories of the hardship immigrants face when moving to America and as a young boy, and so I knew this move must've been very traumatic Mikey. While he was recounting the story, Mikey would occasionally make a joke and lighten the mood. His behavior caught me off guard. There I was sobbing like my pet just died, and Mikey's sharing his story with joy radiating from his heart.

"What's wrong with you?" I asked him, "How can you lighten a deep and painful story like that?" He looked at me and said, "Trust me Allison, I spent many years crying, and back then, that's what I needed to do as part of my healing process. However, I've come to a place of acceptance of my past. I'm no longer hurt by it, instead, I have so much gratitude for the lessons I learned during those long and tough years!"

I realized that Mikey wasn't downplaying or undermining his past by making light of it. Rather, he was in a place of complete surrender to his past and thus, all of the negative emotions he had related to it had disappeared. Negative emotions can only stay for as long as we refuse to confront them. Mikey's honesty in confronting his fear, anger, and confusion about his earliest memories of living in the U.S. caused him to triumph over these emotions and regain control over his life.

The message of this book is that healing is possible for you. Make a commitment right now to look at your life differently, more positively, and spread the love that overflows within you!

CHAPTER 1:

UNDERSTANDING EMOTIONAL TRAUMA

A traumatic event is any incident that causes emotional, physical, psychological, or spiritual harm in your life. As a result of experiencing this trauma, you may feel threatened, anxious, vulnerable, or fearful. In some cases, trauma can cause people to freeze, go numb, emotionally detach, or socially withdraw, temporarily changing who they are and how they interact with the world around them.

Some examples of traumatic events include:

- Going through a divorce or witnessing your parents getting divorced.
- The death of loved ones, close friends, or pets.
- A physical injury caused by a car accident or physical assault.
- Serious or chronic illness.
- Going in for surgery or life after surgery.
- Witnessing natural disasters.
- Acts of war and terrorism.
- Sexual abuse, like child molestation, sexual harassment, or rape.

- Relocating to a new location.
- Losing a job.
- Parental abandonment.
- Going to prison.
- Emotional and physical abuse.

People respond to trauma in many different ways. This is because what one person classifies as traumatic, another may not find to be traumatic at all. For example, Macy's response to the dysfunctional household she grew up in may be different to somebody else's response, who experienced a similar traumatic event. Perhaps this particular person had access to a social worker at the time or had really supportive friends or relatives to confide in.

Even though Macy didn't show any visible signs of the trauma, she had emotional reactions that came as a result of the emotional impact of her dysfunctional home environment. Some of the emotional reactions I remember seeing were:

- Irritability. If Macy felt misunderstood, she would quickly snap and express her frustration. This was because she would try to hold in her tears for so long, but when she had reached her breaking point (which may have happened often) she would release the emotions she suppressed for so long.
- Sudden and dramatic mood changes. On some days, I would see Macy in a jovial and happy-go-lucky state, but after discussing a topic or bringing up a sensitive topic, she would show signs of being uncomfortable.
- Anxiety and nervousness. Whenever Macy and I would go out for ice cream or window shopping at the mall, she'd feel intimidated by the new environment and would panic when coming in close contact with other people.
- Provoked. When I couldn't make time to see Macy, she would find it difficult to understand why I couldn't see her. Many

times she thought maybe it was because I didn't want to spend time with her.
- Denial. Macy didn't know how to begin processing the strong emotions she was feeling. She was afraid of coming to terms with some of the reminders from her past.

Traumatic Stress from Childhood

As far as I am aware, I don't think Macy was speaking to any professional counsellor about her experiences, at the time. Perhaps a counsellor may have told Macy that as a child, she suffered from childhood traumatic stress because she was exposed to one or more traumatic events in her life and developed emotional reactions that affected her behaviors. While Macy didn't develop any substance abuse problems, many children who grow up with traumatic stress may abuse drugs, alcohol, or engage in risky sexual behaviors.

Many of us experience stress in our day-to-day lives. Our stressors vary from the unmoving traffic in the mornings, to not having enough money to buy gas so we can get to work! Our stressors may impact our mood, cause us to feel insecure about who we are and where we're going, or make us want to curl up in a ball and hide from the world. However, children experience stress differently, especially when it comes to trauma-related stress. For them, traumatic stress interferes with their day-to-day lives, to the extent that it can alter their identity and ability to form relationships with others. What's worse is that there is no age at which children are immune to the effects of traumatic stress; each child's response will vary depending on their developmental level.

The legacy of the traumatic experience lives on within the child and echoes into adulthood. The legacy of trauma may manifest as emotional triggers or reminders that are linked to the traumatic event, its consequences, or the aftermath. Adults who experienced childhood trauma could be reminded by revisiting their family home, seeing a person, celebrating an anniversary, or listening to a conversation.

Physical reactions may also serve as reminders. For example, a rapid heart rate or bodily sensation may trigger the memory of the painful experience.

The Signs and Symptoms of PTSD

Post-traumatic stress disorder (PTSD) consists of a cluster of symptoms that begin (and in many cases persist) after you have survived the traumatic incident. In the same way that not everyone will develop PTSD immediately after the trauma, the PTSD symptoms that each individual experiences will vary too. Nonetheless, PTSD symptoms usually persist for at least a month, however, they may continue for many years. In the case of most trauma survivors, these PTSD symptoms represent the survivor's first encounters or struggle with anxiety.

Below are some of the most common PTSD symptoms (not all of them may apply to you):

- Intense feelings of discomfort or grief when reminded about the traumatic event.
- Physical reactions when reminded of the traumatic event (may include vomiting, nausea, migraines, heart palpitations, or sweating).
- Visual and invasive memories of the trauma.
- Mental flashbacks that make you feel as though the trauma is happening all over again.
- Nightmares of the painful incident or other frightening dreams.
- Loss of appetite.
- Loss of interest in social activities you used to love.
- Feeling emotionally detached from people.
- Sense of being cursed; not having a positive outlook on life.
- Difficult remembering certain details of the traumatic event.

What saddens me is that I saw Macy displaying some of these PTSD symptoms, but since she wasn't aware of them herself (or struggled to articulate them), I felt I could do very little to help her. There are so many people who know what they're feeling but have a difficult time expressing their feelings into words. For example, they may feel irritable but will become overwhelmed by their irritability, they decide to walk away or become silent. Although expressing feelings may seem like a small step, it can help one confront and understand how one feels. Below are some examples of how my friend could have expressed what she felt inside:

- "I don't want to think or talk about my past."
- "I can't stop thinking about my past."
- "I feel like I'm going insane."
- "I keep having random panic attacks."
- "I feel like it just happened yesterday."
- "I don't want to go to social events anymore."
- "I don't feel like socializing with my friends anymore."
- "I feel empty inside."
- "I don't have any more love to give."
- "I don't feel safe anywhere."
- "I don't trust people anymore."
- "My life isn't normal."
- "I'm not the person I used to be"
- "I can't remember what happened to me"
- "I don't know where this feeling comes from"
- "I keep having nightmares"

The Connection Between PTSD and Self-Isolation

We had a tradition at college among a group of friends to go out for half-price pizza at a local pizza shop every Friday night. As much as we loved bargain pizza (although it tasted like bargain pizza), we kept this tradition going because it allowed us to catch up with one another and meet new people. Macy knew where to find me on Friday nights, yet she preferred to catch up on school work, which I dearly admired! Nevertheless, I would always extend the invite because I thought it would be a great way for her to meet people who shared the same interests as her. I only learned years later that by constantly nagging her about going out, I may have been pressing against one of her boundaries and making her feel uncomfortable. I take this as a lesson learned!

I had misinterpreted Macy's avoidance of social interactions as her being introverted, but after months of getting to know her, I knew this not to be true! Then, I thought she didn't enjoy meeting new people because she lacked confidence. Once again, this wasn't true, because the Macy I knew could chat up a storm, make me laugh, and seemed quite comfortable with who she was.

It was only later in life when I listened to a podcast speaking about the relationship between PTSD and self-isolation that Macy's avoidance of social interactions made perfect sense! In essence, social isolation refers to the tendency of someone to isolate themselves from others or completely remove themselves from social contexts. Instead of going to parties, traveling, taking on new hobbies, or visiting friends and family, the individual decides to spend time alone.

While it's normal (and necessary) for people to want to spend time alone, especially when they're spending most of their day surrounded by people, it's unhealthy for people to completely retreat into themselves. In other words, craving solitude can be a healthy practice of self-care, but self-isolation can be a symptom underlying mental illnesses, like anxiety, depression, or chronic stress disorder.

The podcast host explained that for a person living with PTSD, self-isolation can become a form of self-preservation. For instance, when Macy was alone or spending time indoors with me, she felt less emotionally triggered, and, in a way, safe. For her, the world was a very scary place and the only way she could protect herself was by staying within the parameters of what she found comforting. Her small dorm room was her safe haven, but outside of those four corners, she felt out of control.

Self-isolation was also the result of Macy feeling extremely lonely, misunderstood, and abandoned. She felt as if she was the only kid who had such a painful childhood and that all the other kids at college wouldn't be able to relate to her experience. Thus, she feared that by interacting with people, she would have to constantly explain her feelings and watch as everybody looked at her like she was strange or different. Therefore, being alone seemed like the safest and most convenient option for Macy, even though I'm pretty sure she sometimes craved a bargain pizza!

The Connection Between PTSD and Dissociation

There's a strong link between PTSD and dissociative disorders. In fact, many researchers believe that long-term trauma is the root cause of many dissociative disorders (Tull, 2019). Dissociation becomes an unhealthy coping mechanism that allows trauma survivors to distance themselves from the memory of unbearable trauma. They do this by disconnecting from their thoughts, feelings, memories, perceptions, or sense of identity. Some examples may include daydreaming, zoning out in the middle of a conversation, or not remembering certain events.

Dissociative disorders involve a degree of dissociation that interferes with a person's well-being, daily routines and activities, and lifestyle. For example, a person with a dissociative disorder may be absent-minded at work, which may compromise their work quality or negatively impact their productivity. Another example of dissociation is when a person emotionally detaches themselves from others, thereby harming their personal relationships. Below are just a few types of dissociative disorders:

- Dissociative amnesia: Having memory loss as it pertains to certain periods of time in your life or important events.

- Dissociative fugue: Mentally wandering off and not having any recollection of a memory or period of time.
- Depersonalization: The sense of being separated from your body and feeling as though you were experiencing your body or feelings from an observer's position.
- Dissociative identity disorder: When a person's personality splits into multiple personalities (formerly known as multiple personality syndrome).

In the initial period following a traumatic event, dissociation may be used as a coping strategy. The trauma survivor may use it as a self-protective technique to mentally distance themselves or escape from reliving painful experiences. This is especially true in the case of children who experience or live in traumatic conditions and cannot physically take themselves out of that environment.

Dissociation without any real and present threat may prove to be dangerous. It can interfere with a person's ability to relate and bond with others, their performance at work, and their ability to set meaningful goals and achieve them. Dissociating from a non-threatening situation may also cause the person to tolerate dysfunctional relationships or self-destructive behaviors that need to be addressed and changed.

The Connection Between PTSD and Relationships

According to the National Center (2020), trauma survivors with PTSD tend to experience problems in their intimate relationships. Some of the symptoms that are related to PTSD interfere with the way a survivor builds and maintains trust in relationships, or their willingness to be emotionally vulnerable. Some of the problems a person with PTSD may experience include:
- The loss of interest in social or sexual activities. This may cause the survivor's friends or romantic partner to feel hurt,

alienated, or frustrated, which may turn into resentment for the survivor.
- Feeling irritable or guarded around others. The survivor may not be able to relax in social situations or enjoy intimacy without being tense.
- Difficulty falling asleep or frequently having nightmares. This may disrupt the sleeping patterns of both the survivor and their partner and could make sleeping together difficult.
- Having trauma memories or reminders that make you feel frightened, anxious, or grieved. This could make living with a trauma survivor feel like a war zone or living in constant fear of emotional outbursts.
- Having constant flashbacks and reminders can also interfere with the survivor's ability to learn and concentrate. They may also find it difficult to listen carefully, follow instructions, or make cooperative decisions.

Many trauma survivors have reported feeling a deep-rooted sense of vulnerability and betrayal that stands in the way of them building genuine connections with others. Opening up about themselves, trusting another person, or being sexually intimate may feel dangerous and threatening. In their minds, they think, "I trusted someone before and they violated me. What if this person has the same intentions?"

Throughout our friendship, Macy found it difficult to let her guard down, but I'm one of the lucky few who had the privilege of getting close to her. I guess I earned it by not trying to push her to open up and showing her, through our interactions, that I didn't intend on causing her any pain. My friendship with Macy lasted for about 2 years and a few months. We grew apart because our relationship was starting to negatively impact my own mental health, and she found another trusted friend, so I was relieved to know she was in good hands.

Like any young woman, I had a few insecurities of my own so I understood the battle Macy was going through. No one could have prepared either of us for the kinds of emotional pain we would need to resolve in our adult lives, and so I knew my friend was dealing with it the best she could. I was still rooting for Macy and I would often think about her when watching an episode of Friends. We had such a special friendship and she taught me more about mental health than I could have learned from any course.

Although I didn't tell Macy that I internally decided to distance myself, she soon caught on and immediately thought it was because I didn't like her anymore. I tried hard assuring her that it wasn't the case; that I actually truly loved her and was worried for her. I expressed how much I wanted her to prioritize her mental health and try to begin standing on her own two feet to face the battles that she crosses in life, because healing comes from within. I referred her to my counselor, gave her a big squeeze, and told her to take care of herself.

Reflecting back on my friendship with Macy, I'm grateful for the lessons she taught me about the importance of healing from trauma. Below are six lessons I walked away with from my friendship with Macy:

Lesson 1: PTSD Is a Real Illness.

Many people like to look at the symptoms of PTSD and see them as bad, disruptive behavior or the survivor's way of seeking attention or "acting out." PTSD is a crippling anxiety disorder that occurs after a traumatic period or event in someone's life. Just as someone cannot snap out of depression, they also cannot control their PTSD-induced emotional reactions. Most people with PTSD aren't triggered all of the time; in fact, there are moments where they remember who they are and radiate so much light and joy. However, the unexpected flashbacks, reminders, or triggers could ruin the moment for both of you.

Lesson 2: People With PTSD Tend to Feel Unlovable.

As much as I reassured Macy that I appreciated her friendship and that I enjoyed our time together, she couldn't help but feel unlovable.

She felt undeserving of our relationship, often asking me, "What do you see in me?" but the truth was that I saw a beautiful, kind, nurturing, and incredibly goofy person who was everything I'd want in a friend.

Lesson 3: There Are Treatment Options for PTSD.

Many people with PTSD aren't aware that PTSD is treatable. Of course, asking for help is never easy; no one wants to feel like something's wrong with them or that they are different in any way. If seeking treatment is a pathway to better mental health, then it's worth making the effort to get in touch with a therapist, or call the SAMHSA National Hotline at 1-800-662-HELP (4357).

Lesson 4: Love Isn't Always Enough.

Saying goodbye to my friend wasn't easy. Even though I was choosing to take time for myself, I still considered her one of my closest buddies. Although I knew she had it a lot harder since battling your own self is one of the most difficult things I can imagine, it was also emotionally exhausting for me to watch as she self-destructed, trying to help, but not being able to; worrying and loving but without any progression. However, we can't always save our loved ones with PTSD from self-destructing. Healing comes from within and no matter how much outside support is given, if one doesn't choose to want to change, there won't be any progress.

Lesson 5: You have to Put Yourself First.

My counselor helped me realize my mental health was my first priority. If I didn't feel good about myself, how could I add value to other people's lives? Caretakers who are in friendships or relationships with people with PTSD forget to take care of themselves. They're more worried about their friend or romantic partner with PTSD than they are about their own health, happiness, and sense of fulfillment in life. I had to learn how to treat myself well first and connect with my own truth and what makes me happy.

Lesson 6: It's OK to Walk Away.

This was perhaps the hardest lesson to learn because walking away made me feel so guilty. I thought to myself: "Who will take care of Macy when I'm gone?" or "Who will understand her emotional outbursts as well as I did?" I walked away not because I didn't love her anymore, but because she needed to address very serious health issues that were getting in the way of our friendship. We just couldn't continue being friends under those circumstances without me falling into a depression or developing some kind of mental illness too. Time away from her was what we both needed, and I'm glad I made that decision.

The Stages of Healing

There is no time frame or deadline as to when you'll stop feeling traumatized. A traumatic event can leave you psychologically wounded for months or many years. It's important to show compassion to yourself as you process the pain, confusion, and anger caused by a traumatic incident or childhood trauma. The most important message for you to remember is that healing is possible for you when you're ready to travel down that road.

Recovery from trauma is such a personal process and thus, it will look differently for everyone. For instance, your unique ability to heal from past trauma depends on various factors including your beliefs and perceptions, your level of resilience, the strength of your support system, and other psychological triggers you may have experienced before the traumatic event.

Recovery from trauma is a rewarding process that involves learning how to live in the present moment without being troubled by your past.

You may still experience flashbacks or reminders once in a while, however, these flashbacks don't carry an emotional charge like they used to. In other words, the memory of your past no longer has control over your present emotions, and as a result, you're able to forgive yourself, make peace with your past, build healthy relationships, and feel a sense of freedom!

CHAPTER 2:

SAFETY, STABILIZATION, AND OVERCOMING DYSREGULATION

People who have been affected by trauma often feel unsafe in their own bodies and in their relationships with others. Once again, there's no timeline indicating when a trauma survivor will feel in control of their own bodies again. It may take a few weeks for those with acute trauma, and months or years for those who have experienced recurring trauma in their lives.

When we think of safety, I'm referring to more than the relationship with the outside world. Generally, after experiences of trauma, survivors may develop guilt about being able to provide safety for themselves (Fredrek, 2018). They believe that it was their own action or inaction that caused them to fall victim to abuse or violence. Of course, this isn't true, however, this surmounting level of guilt makes survivors feel exposed and constantly threatened.

When Mikey, my former work colleague, realized that his experience of the United States wouldn't be as glamorous as he had seen in magazines, his heart sank. Back in Mexico, Mikey and his family lived in a city in central Mexico called Queretaro. His father had built a successful business selling car parts to other car dealerships in the surrounding cities. In 2008, when the United States went into a recession, it significantly impacted the Mexican economy. It became too expensive for Mikey's father to run his business, and since they desperately needed a source of income, he decided to sell the business. The family was able to live on the cash reserves for another year, with assistance from Mikey's mother who was a teacher at a nearby school. However, near the end of 2009, the family was struggling to make ends meet.

At the time, Mikey was 14 years old. His friends in his community would jokingly call him a "fresa," which was a term used to refer to a person who came from a rich family and lived a comfortable lifestyle. The truth was that Mikey had it better than most of his friends. His family would travel on vacation outside Mexico, his father would frequently gift him with the latest tech gadgets, and he wore the latest designer clothing. Even though the recession publicly impacted Mikey's father through the collapse of his business, it also left a significant impact on Mikey.

Over the course of a few months, the life he was accustomed to changed drastically. His father was now a stay-at-home dad who would cook, clean, and run errands for the family. This was humiliating for Mikey, who had always known his father to be the world's best provider. He didn't want his friends to hang out at his place anymore because he thought they would mock his father and question his family's financial position. All of a sudden, he felt responsible for keeping this secret to himself, and for protecting the reputation of his family.

The pressure of keeping this secret meant that Mikey spent less time with his friends and more time alone at home. For him, home was the safest place on earth. No one could judge him or his family at home because no one saw what took place behind those walls. Spending time alone became the new normal, and this led to a period of depression. He felt sad, hopeless, and fearful for his family's future, but he didn't know how to help. He was young and still had a few more years of school to complete before he could find a job and contribute to the family household.

Mikey felt powerless in saving his family's financial situation. He also felt a sense of guilt, having been spoiled by his parents throughout his childhood, yet not able to help them in their greatest time of need. His world felt unsafe, and anxiety became a part of his daily life. His mind was plagued with "What if" scenarios, regrets, and self-judgment. At the time, he didn't have anyone who could tell him that he was suffering from PTSD. His parents, suffering from an equal amount of traumatic stress, didn't see anything worrying in his reclusive behavior.

Mike's parents took him to see a therapist, fearing that their home situation could negatively impact his mental health. One of the first lessons he learned about recovery was the importance of regaining a sense of safety. Below are some of the actionable recommendations the therapist provided.

Step 1: Re-establish Bodily Safety

One of the characteristics of trauma is that it dysregulates the body. It shifts a person's energy levels around from the normal baseline to extreme feelings of hyperarousal or hypoarousal. For example, a trauma survivor may become overwhelmed by daily activities or feel emotions intensely, or, alternatively, they may become lethargic and feel a sense of emptiness.

Mikey felt overwhelmed in his body. He often thought about running away from home or at the very least, hiding in his room. He was too young to drink alcohol, but if he was a few years older at the time, I'm pretty sure he would find ways of medicating his pain away. The dysregulation in his body also made him want to escape mentally and try by all means not to think about the financial woes his family was experiencing. He would often lie on his bed, daydreaming about the lifestyle he used to have. This provided pleasurable feelings for him and made coping with the stress at home bearable.

Unknowingly, Mikey was finding ways to separate himself from his bodily experience and to numb the pain he was feeling. It ultimately led to him separating himself from the undesirable sensory input coming through his body. When he spoke, he seemed to be doing well, however, if his parents paid close attention, they would see the physical symptoms of hypoarousal written all over his body.

Bessel van der Kolk, author of the book *The Body Keeps the Score: Brain, Mind, and Body in the Healing of Trauma*, wrote about the experience that trauma survivors go through when they separate themselves from their bodies. In his book, he says "[T]heir bodies are constantly bombarded by visceral warning signs, and, in an attempt to control these processes, they often become expert at ignoring their gut feelings and in numbing awareness of what is played out inside. They learn to hide from their selves" (McAllister, 2017).

Splitting from the "self" seems to be the safest option available at the time, since the present experience is seen as threatening. However, over time, the split from "self" causes the trauma survivor to become their own worst enemy. They take on a critical approach in assessing their lives and view the traumatized self as inappropriate, humiliating, weak, unlovable, worthless, or unacceptable. They start to believe that they fall short of providing the kind of security they need in life. In extreme cases, the survivor may even blame themselves for not doing anything to prevent the trauma from occurring.

The survivor also develops critical ways of thinking about themselves and others. Their friends or family members may comment that they've become cold, detached, or extremely judgmental. They may also lose passion for the hobbies or social activities they took part in before the trauma occurred. Moreover, in their bid to re-establish safety, they may develop very rigid and unforgiving boundaries and standards in their life, and require others to follow and respect them. In Miky's case, he came up with a rule that he would only go out to play with his friends on Saturdays. During the week, he wanted to focus solely on school work so that he could improve his grades (and hopefully qualify for college scholarships in a few years), and Sundays he dedicated himself to spending time with his family—even though he never left his room on Sundays, anyways.

Re-establishing bodily safety requires survivors to revisit the place within them that feels frightened. The only way they can come back to their bodies is by confronting the overwhelming emotional triggers they feel as a result of the trauma. Instead of mentally escaping when they feel a rush of strong emotions coming, they would need to stand and feel the emotions until the warning signs go off. Accessing uncomfortable emotions and allowing them to flow through the body can provide an experience of healing. It can also show the survivor that they're strong enough to handle and confront pain, which encourages feelings of safety in their bodies.

Mikey finally summoned enough courage to face the overwhelming emotions he was running away from. He started by changing his perspective on these strong and invasive feelings. For example, instead of perceiving his anger or confusion as a sign of weakness, he saw both as natural and appropriate responses to the sudden financial crisis in their household. Changing his perspective helped him neutralize the emotions, making them less intimidating. He told himself that every time he would feel anger rising within him, he would simply declare, "This anger is welcome for as long as it wants to be acknowledged." On some days, he would feel angry for hours, and on other days, it would come and go in waves. Nonetheless, he was able to regain sensation in his body and feel every emotion that demanded to be felt.

He also found grounding in nature. He began taking short walks in the afternoons to get some fresh air and take in the beauty of nature around him. These walks also helped to bring a sense of calm over him and soothe his mind. He always felt rejuvenated after a walk. After telling his parents about how helpful it was for him, they started walking with him and it became a time for the family to reconnect with one another.

Step 2: Re-establish Physical Safety

After a traumatic experience, it may be difficult to regain the connection between mind and body. One another factor that may interfere with this process is when a survivor feels threatened in their environment. As long as Mikey locked himself in his room or isolated himself at home, his mind would always perceive his environment and social interactions as being threatening. His therapist encouraged him to adopt coping strategies that would help him perceive his environment as being a safe space.

At first, Mikey insisted that he felt safe at home and that there was nothing the therapist had to worry about. The therapist saw his state of denial as being a teaching moment. She replied, "If you truly felt safe at home, why would you only come out of your room to grab a plate of food? Why would you avoid interactions with your parents, or watching TV together as a family? It seems to me, Mikey, that you are afraid of being re-traumatized by leaving your bedroom. You fear that if you strike a conversation with your mother that she'll tell you about the stress she's experiencing, and this might put you over the edge."

Mikey was old enough to understand the message the therapist was getting across and unfortunately, he couldn't deny anything she was saying. It was true; Mikey feared seeing the look of hopelessness on his parents' face or overhearing a conversation about a lack of money. The therapist comforted Mikey, telling him that it was possible to create a safe space at home, although it would be a slow process.

The first thing Mikey learned about creating a safe physical space was that it wasn't about locking doors. In the context of trauma, creating physical safety meant the ability to build an environment that allowed his mind and body to manage emotional discomfort. For example, even though Mikey wasn't in danger at home, he felt emotionally vulnerable every time he stepped out of his bedroom. Part of creating a safe space at home would involve finding ways of feeling safe to be himself at home and to freely let his guard down. Some of the strategies offered by the therapist include:

Creating a Coping Kit

She told Mikey to find an old shoe box in the house and decorate it with glitter, fabric, paper, beads, and any other kinds of material he could find. The goal of decorating the box was to reduce the feelings of anxiety associated with the exercise, as well as provide a stimulating and soothing activity for him to do. After decorating the box, the therapist asked Mikey to insert random items that made him feel at ease. There were no wrong or right items, as long as every item was useful in some way to offer Mikey support when feeling emotionally triggered. Mikey enjoyed the task of decorating his shoebox and once complete, he added a stress ball, a photo of him and his family on vacation, a list of positive affirmations, and his favorite Bible scriptures.

Creating a Coping Corner

His therapist also advised Mikey to find a private area in his home (apart from his bedroom) that he could retreat to when he felt overwhelmed. This would be a place where he felt inspired, at peace, and most understood. The therapist encouraged Mikey to dress the place up by adding candles, a blanket, or positive distractions like art supplies. Mikey was excited to take on this mini-project. He chose to create his coping corner in an empty garden shed. No one had gone in the shed for many years so his parents had no problem with allowing him to use it. Mikey cleaned out the shed and remodeled it into a mini living area. The end result looked like a photo you'd find on Pinterest. Whenever he visited his coping corner, the negative thoughts in his mind would disappear. He would focus instead on painting his emotions or lying down on his beanbag chair and listening to his favorite musician.

Incorporating Physical Exercise

The therapist told Mikey that staying physically healthy was an important element in him feeling safe at home. Exercise would improve his overall mental wellness, boost his mood, and cause him to feel at peace at home. Since he enjoyed being outdoors, the counselor suggested that he finds a few exercises that he would perform on the lawn a few times per week. The goal here wasn't to build muscle or get in shape, but instead to increase the heartbeat and break a sweat. After a few weeks of exercise, Mikey developed a love for pilates. That became his go-to routine whenever he had 15 minutes to spare for a workout.

Part of re-establishing physical safety meant that Mikey also needed to regain a feeling of safety in his relationships. Having a healthy and supportive social network would help Mikey feel a sense of belonging in a larger community of people who loved him and were available to be a shoulder to cry on. Being connected to others would also help Mikey understand that many families experience financial instability and therefore, it wasn't anything he needed to be ashamed about. If he paid attention to some of the things his friends were sharing, he would remember that two of his friends spoke about their parents losing their jobs due to the recession.

The therapist asked Mikey if there was any reason for him to see his friends as untrustworthy. His reply was a quick, "No." Her follow-up question was, "What makes you feel as though you cannot trust them?" He told the therapist that his mistrust was largely due to feeling as though his friends would mock him. For many years, he was known as the "rich kid" and his family was seen as the "rich family." Mikey thought his friends would make fun of him and tease his current lifestyle, which was strikingly different from how he used to live. The therapist sympathized with Mikey's perception of his friends, but broke the silence with the following question, "Have your friends ever given you a reason to believe they would mock your personal struggles?"

Mikey thought about this question for a while. His friends loved joking around and making light of certain situations. However, there was never a time where they made a mockery of personal situations. Mikey recalled a time one of his friends fell off his skateboard and injured his knee badly. Instead of laughing at his fall, all of them ran to go and see if the injured friend was okay. Together, they carried him to the nearest home and asked for warm water and a cloth to disinfect the wound, before carrying him home. He also recalled another time where he forgot to bring packed lunch from home. He mentioned it to his friend group and each of them opened their lunch boxes and gave Mikey a snack that he could eat. By the end of recess, he was full from all of the food his friend's offered him.

The therapist smiled and said, "You see, your friends are not as judgmental as you had thought after all. Who knows of the various ways they could help you if you confided in them?" Mikey looked at her and simply smiled back. The therapist proceeded to give him a few strategies on re-establishing safety in his friendships:

1. Know Who You Can Call

Within friend groups, there are those we are closest to and others we only speak to when we happen to see them. The therapist asked Mikey to take a piece of paper and a pen and write down the names of the friends he felt closest to. Next to each name, the therapist asked him to write down the reason why he felt so close to them. Perhaps he could easily open up to these friends or they knew his family history better than anyone else. His therapist then asked him to write down in which emergencies he would need to call each friend. For example, if he was overwhelmed by negative thoughts he might choose a particular friend over another.

2. Use Creativity to Stay Connected

The therapist knew that Mikey had set up a rule to only see his friends on Saturdays. She respected his rule, although it didn't mean that he couldn't connect with them in other ways throughout the week. Technology has made it easier to connect with friends without having to physically see them. Mikey was quite tech-savvy and liked the idea of hosting weekly Zoom conference calls with his friends. Not only could they catch up on the shows each one of them was watching, but they could also discuss schoolwork and help each other academically.

3. Offer to be Someone Else's Shoulder to Cry On

Relationships are all about reciprocity. If you want a friend to check-in on you, you need to regularly check-in on your friend. The therapist encouraged Mikey to offer support to his friends because they might be experiencing challenging situations too. By offering support, Mikey would also open himself to receive support in return. There's nothing more healing than offering advice that also heals and encourages you!

Step 3: Re-establish Emotional Stability

Before their first counseling session together, the therapist asked Mikey to prepare a letter describing how he felt inside. Mikey was at first hesitant to prepare this letter because he thought the therapist would judge how miserable he was. She reassured him that the letter wasn't so that she could criticize him, it would help him see how far he'd come when their sessions had reached an end. Below is a copy of his letter:

> *Pain. This is what I constantly feel in my mind and body. I can't remember the last time I slept without a headache or woke up without my stomach cramping. I thought stress was only meant to remain in the mind; I didn't expect it to reach my body.*

I don't know what else to write about. There's nothing else I feel right now. Ever since my life changed, I became someone I didn't recognize. I don't like who I am right now. I'm heartless and inconsiderate. I'm also lazy and would rather sleep in the whole day than going out with my friends.

I guess I'll reconnect with them once this situation clears up. When we reunite, I'll explain everything. Hopefully, they understand and take me back into the circle. I miss them terribly, but I don't want them to see me like this.

I don't want to see myself like this.

Send help. Please.

She listened as Mikey read his own letter. She praised him for his courage to put his thoughts and feelings in words. Journaling his thoughts and feelings became Mikey's favorite way of releasing pent-up emotions and decluttering his mind. For him, writing was a way of validating what he felt and letting himself know that what he felt was normal. Journaling became one of the strategies he used in re-establishing emotional safety.

Emotional safety isn't about selecting which feelings are appropriate to feel and which ones are inappropriate to feel. In the field of psychology, there is no such thing as a "bad" or "good" emotion. Every emotion can be useful depending on the context. For example, anxiety can be useful when preparing for an exam or before a presentation. It can cause you to concentrate more intensely and operate at your peak. Therefore, there are many instances where feeling anxious may be advantageous. The therapist told Mikey that it doesn't serve him to turn off certain emotions because by cutting off one emotion, you're cutting off all of them.

For example, if he tried to get rid of his anxiety, he would feel numb or detached from his present experience. This means that it would be impossible for him to feel the presence of joy, peace, or satisfaction in his present experience too. The only way to feel and appreciate peace is to know what anxiety feels like. Emotional safety is about honoring all emotions and treating them all as beneficial. It involves learning strategies to regulate your emotions, both in how you treat yourself and others. When you feel emotionally safe, you're able to process strong emotions without reacting negatively to them. For example, you may be in a triggering situation but have tools in place to help you calm your nervous system and bring you to a place of feeling calm and in control. Below are a few self-soothing strategies that the therapist recommended Mikey implement to help him regulate his emotions:

1. Get in Touch With Your Senses

Can you remember the first time you smelled fresh flowers? Or the smell of coffee brewing? What about the taste of warm chocolate chip cookies? Or hearing the loud joyful laughter of a loved one? His therapist told Mikey that his five senses had the potential to heighten his mood when he was mindful of his surroundings. Paying attention to the senses could also help him feel more grounded in the present moment and let go of troubling thoughts about his family situation. Below are a few tips that Mikey was given to engage his senses:

- Smell: Freshly baked treats, lighting a scented candle, spending time in the garden, using fabric softener on clothes and bedding, using scented lotion or wearing a beautiful perfume, breathing in deeply.
- Sight: Reading a book or magazine, watching an informative documentary or cat videos online, watching a TV show as a family, cleaning your bedroom, reorganizing your bedroom in your favorite colors, observing plants in the garden, taking photos of yourself.
- Taste: Eating your favorite meal or dessert (in moderation), focusing on the texture and flavors of food, taking smaller bites

and chewing slowly, having a piece of chocolate, taking a short break to have tea or coffee.
- Sound: Listening to uplifting music, playing a musical instrument, watching a stand-up comedy special, laughing uncontrollably.
- Touch: Wearing light and comfortable clothing, hand painting, washing your hair, cuddling furry animals, squeezing a stress ball.

2. The 5-4-3-2-1 Grounding Technique

This grounding technique helps to bring your mind back into the present moment, especially when you're feeling a sense of panic. The technique goes like this:

- 5-Smell: "I can smell the wooden floors, clean linen, my own cologne, a scented candle, and freshly cut grass."
- 4-Sight: "I can see my bed, dresser, flowers outside, and my desk."
- 3-Taste: "I can taste coffee, toothpaste from the morning, and the flavor of gum."
- 2-Sound: "I can hear the lawnmower and birds chirping."
- 1-Touch: "I feel my clothing."

3. Creating Positive Mantras

When strong emotions are heightened, the brain can easily slip into a loop of negative self-talk. The therapist discussed the benefit of creating positive mantras for Mikey. She said that these mantras are effective in countering negative thoughts by offering truthful affirmations about who he is and what he's capable of. She then asked

Mikey to think of a few Mantras that he could affirm in various situations. Below is his list of mantras:

- I am intelligent.
- I enjoy laughing at my mistakes.
- I am valuable to those around me.
- Even in my weakness, I am strong.
- Failure is feedback.
- This too shall pass.
- I am an overcomer.
- My life is only getting better.
- Everything is working for my highest good.
- I am growing wiser each day.

CHAPTER 3:

REMEMBRANCE, MOURNING, AND COMING TO TERMS WITH TRAUMATIC MEMORIES

I remember some of the times when I decided to speak to Macy about her trauma-induced behaviors. I tried to put it in the kindest way possible that I thought her behaviors may have been related to past events in her life. Her responses would usually be:

"I don't have trauma."

"What I experienced wasn't trauma."

"Most people experience a dysfunctional childhood, I should've been able to cope with mine."

"My life story isn't sad and I'm not sad about it either."

"I'm not upset at my parents or how my childhood turned out."

One of the most difficult things for a trauma survivor to do is admit they're suffering from trauma. There tends to be a general assumption that admitting to suffering from trauma is a sign of weakness or a desperate cry for attention. No one wants to feel as though they don't have a firm grip on their lives, even when they're overwhelmed by their life situation. Even terms like "trauma survivor" can make a victim of trauma feel weak, ashamed, or a sense of failure.

The second stage of recovery from trauma involves remembering and coming to terms with the painful event or period of your life that left you traumatized. This task is impossible when a survivor is still in denial. Denial keeps the survivor in a cycle of negative behavioral patterns and dissociates them from their current life experience. Other people around the survivor may also be in denial about the trauma and may not want the survivor to admit to being traumatized. For example, the immediate family of the survivor may have been keeping the abuse a secret for many years due to protecting the perpetrators involved (who may also be part of the family).

The denial of the trauma absolves everyone of the guilt of having knowledge of the abuse but not doing anything to end it. Survivors may also be afraid of facing backlash from others by admitting to their trauma. They may be accused of lying, promiscuity, or falsely accusing the abuser. This would re-traumatize the survivor and take them back to a place of feeling unsafe in their relationships.

Denial of trauma also occurs when, as part of their coping strategy, the survivor learns how to suppress strong emotions. When a person cannot identify and express difficult emotions, they may be unable to recognize the truth behind their negative thoughts or impulsive behavior. They may claim that their excessive drinking or reckless sexual activities have nothing to do with their painful past.

While it may be difficult for someone who's in denial to see this, there are a few common signs and symptoms of denial that can help you identify it in yourself or in a loved one:

- You avoid talking about the traumatic incident or subject, rather than speaking about it openly.
- You compare your own behaviors to someone else's to convince yourself and others that you don't have a problem.

- You often make unrealistic promises, like "I'll seek counselling tomorrow" or "This is my last drink for good."
- You adamantly refuse to be given advice by others about addressing your self-destructive behaviors.
- You become aggressive, emotional, or defensive when others offer help.
- You blame other people for your current life situation.
- You claim that your behaviors don't affect anybody else.

When you're ready, you can gradually come out of a state of denial by following these five steps:

Step 1: Ask Yourself if You're Ready to Feel

A state of denial doesn't require you to take responsibility for your thoughts and feelings. This may seem like a suitable idea for some, however, it robs you of the ability to truly connect to your life. Learn to take ownership of your thoughts and feelings, without judging yourself for how ugly they seem. Remember that once you confront your negative thoughts and feelings, they have less power to control you. Learn to look, without forming an opinion, and accept that part of being human is having the ability to feel a range of emotions.

Step 2: Look at Your Life With Curiosity

Curiosity can take you further than criticism can. When you look at your life critically, you see memories in black and white. The people in your past are either good or evil and the outcomes of your life are either fulfilling or hopeless. Looking at life in this way can be discouraging, especially because nobody's perfect and life is unfair. Curiosity causes you to look at the same memories with an open mind. Instead of trying to differentiate between the good and bad person, you're more interested in your own emotional reactions and how your perceptions impacted the relationships you had with those around you. Curiosity allows you to trace the roots of your denial or pain so that you can fix the problem at its core.

Step 3: Listen to What Others Have to Say

One of the symptoms of denial is being defensive toward those who offer guidance or support. Thus, part of healing denial involves learning how to listen to what other people think and feel about your situation. Once again, you will need to adopt a curious mind so that you can take in what others say without feeling attacked or judged. Choose people who are close to you and trust that they have good intentions for what they decide to share with you. Think about their responses and see how they might be right in how they analyzed your situations.

Step 4: Learn to Accept Yourself

Those who use denial as a coping mechanism tend to also deny themselves through dissociation. They develop an abusive relationship with themselves, which often leads to self-destructive patterns of behavior or addictions. Learning to accept and love yourself is a journey, but the best place to start is by being honest with what you need in your life. You may need financial stability, proper shelter, a job that you're passionate about, or to reconnect with your family or start a family of your own. Make it your life's mission to prioritize these needs because they're yours and you deserve to live a life that makes you happy!

Step 5: Let Go of Feelings of Shame

It's impossible to recover from denial when you're still feeling shameful about your past. Shame causes you to hide certain aspects of your life out of fear that they are too undesirable or complicated for anyone to accept. It eats away at your self-esteem and makes you think less of yourself. By accepting the complete truth about your past and who you are today, shame will no longer have a place in your life. Your truth is your unique life story that has made you the strong, wise, responsible, and kind person you are today. Embrace everything that makes you authentically yourself and let others get to know the real you.

Making Peace With Your Inner Child

A popular term that's been embraced by the self-help movement is the "inner child." It describes an almost childlike aspect of your personality that can take over when you're faced with challenging situations. It's important to not confuse this term with an attitude of childishness; the inner child symbolizes the younger versions of yourself who have either healed or are still wounded from past experiences. Your inner child can also embody both negative and positive aspects of the pain and joy you experience as a child.

One striking attribute related to the inner child is how it stores repressed emotions. If you were rewarded for "good" behavior and punished for "bad" behavior, your inner child may hold feelings of rejection, sadness, or anger that you couldn't process when you were younger. If you experienced abuse at a young age, you probably learned how to hide the pain, however, hiding it didn't release it—the pain was stored in your subconscious mind and triggered whenever the "child" in you felt threatened.

The more I learned about the concept of the inner child, the more I understood Macy's emotional outbursts. Growing up in such a dysfunctional home environment must have impacted her beyond what I could see with my naked eye. Since she couldn't escape from home, she had to learn how to normalize the emotional abuse caused by her parents. Her inner child probably saw this behavior as the safest way to exist in such a volatile environment. However, later in her life, when she had left home and gone to college, Macy's inner child became resentful of having to live through such a painful childhood. This resentment was expressed through various tactics and the negative beliefs she had adopted about herself and her life. In a way, the inner child was demanding for someone to make amends and take responsibility for the pain that was inflicted.

Macy felt unsafe as a child because her parents' love was conditional. She had to perform well at school or find ways of being a "good girl" to receive positive reinforcement. It also didn't help to see her parents constantly fighting (and then making up a few hours later). She learned that love wasn't guaranteed in relationships and that she could survive without needing love from anyone else. These thoughts and feelings caused deep wounds that reemerged in her adult life. Many adults face the same challenges as Macy did with building healthy relationships with others due to the deep-rooted beliefs they accepted in their childhood. Below are some of the common ways some children are made to feel unsafe in their childhood:

- Some children are taught that their opinions don't matter.
- Some children are disciplined when attempting to speak up for themselves or present a different opinion to their caregivers.
- Some children are given restrictions on how they should play and what is considered acceptable or unacceptable play.
- Some children aren't allowed to ask questions or be curious about the world.
- Some children are disciplined when they express strong emotions such as fear or anger.
- Some children are humiliated by their parents.
- Some children are beaten when they make mistakes.
- Some children are made to feel responsible for making their parents happy or doing everything in their power to relieve stress from their parents.
- Some children were not given physical affection, like hugs or kisses, from their parents.

Thinking about how influential Macy's inner child was in shaping her experience of the world, I couldn't help but wonder the many ways my inner child had shaped how I saw the world. I cannot say that my childhood was perfect, even though I was fortunate enough to come from a healthy and stable upbringing. My parents were active in raising us and teaching us valuable life principles. I'm the oldest of four children and all of us turned out alright. However, my inner child still held something against my past. I realized this when I reflected on how I felt responsible to take care of Macy, even though she wasn't great at taking care of me.

I was quite happy to play the role of caretaker knowing that my relationship with Macy wasn't reciprocated. I began looking back at my childhood to find clues for why I acted like that. Again, my home life was healthy and I didn't suffer from anything most children or teenagers don't suffer from. Eventually, after weeks of analyzing various childhood memories, I figured it out. I was the first-born child in my family and growing up, I always felt like that role carried a lot of pressure. There was a significant age gap between my siblings and me, so when they were children, my mother would often ask me to help out with them. I didn't mind helping out at all. In fact, I grew to love it because every time I would help one of my younger siblings, my parents would find a way to acknowledge my efforts.

When my siblings became teenagers, I felt responsible to support them the best way I could. Since I had already experienced the horrors of puberty and the experience of high school, I found myself calling them constantly to check up on how they were doing. I was pouring out my love and support to my younger siblings out of fear that if I didn't encourage them, they might fall into the temptations of youth. Looking back, this was an irrational fear. There was no way I could prevent a rebellious teenager from doing whatever the heck they wanted.

I learned to be a caretaker long before I met Macy. From a very young age, I had conditioned myself to put the needs of those I loved first. Unfortunately, this also meant that I would come across friends who were comfortable being taken care of but hardly paid any attention to me! Acknowledging the ways in which my inner child was impacted during childhood meant that I could bring healing to the part of me that wanted to take care of others but neglected to take care of myself. It also meant that I could finally tell my inner child what it was waiting so long to hear:

Dear Inner Child, I Love You

I love you as you are. You don't need to perform in any way to earn my love and affection. You don't need to take care of people so that you can feel responsible. The way you've been able to bounce back through various obstacles in life is enough to tell me that you're extremely responsible. You deserve to be loved with the same intensity you love others. I intend on showing you this immense love, without requiring you to do anything to qualify for it. From now on, I will take care of you as well as I've taken care of my younger siblings and friends. It's your time to receive all of the warmth and compassion I have to offer!

Dear Inner Child, I Hear You

I've heard your petitions loud and clear. I apologize for thinking you weren't hurt by my childhood in any way. I respect how you feel and I'm determined to right my wrongs. I understand your need for support. For so many years, I've been a shoulder to cry on for other people but neglected your pain. I promise to hear you out whenever you signal that you're feeling upset. I promise to listen to your grievances and find ways to offer you healing.

Dear Inner Child, I Forgive You

I forgive you for the pressure you made me feel to care for other people. Sometimes, I felt exhausted but pushed myself to get up and show up for others. I would stay on the phone for hours listening to other people's problems, knowing that I had my own personal problems that nobody knew about. I forgive you for making me grow up too quickly. I love my siblings, but I should've let my parents raise them, so I could enjoy my childhood. I missed out on so many parties because of babysitting and unfortunately, I can't relive those years again. I don't hold this against you. You didn't know any better. At least from now on, we can make better decisions that honor my own happiness.

The Energetic Nature of Trauma

Macy experienced ongoing trauma which made her stuck on fight-or-flight mode most of the time. She was constantly on guard, waiting for another life-shattering event to occur. Even though there were no real threats in her environment, the imagined threats were enough to cause physiological reactions in her body.

I remember one summer rushing Macy to the hospital because she had fainted in her dorm room. I was so concerned about her well-being and I wanted to make sure nothing serious had happened. The nurses examined her and found her blood pressure was low. The saddest part about the whole ordeal was when Macy insisted that no one call her parents. She said it would cause them a lot of unnecessary stress. Looking back, I think Macy was more afraid that her parents would respond in an unloving way and embarrass her in front of the hospital staff. We agreed to not call her parents and I spent the day with her doing some of the activities we both loved.

There was also an occasion where Macy complained a lot about her muscles aching and the constant migraines that would interfere with her sight and ability to concentrate. Her quick solution was to take pills but I thought we could try and find alternative ways to treat her physical aches and pains. According to studies, trauma rewires the brain and activates an ongoing stress response. When the stress response is activated, the body assumes the person is in serious danger and goes into shock or freezes. In this state, the body is vulnerable to contracting illnesses since it's not functioning optimally.

When animals in the animal kingdom suffer trauma, they tend to "shake off" the shock or freeze response (Shaw, 2019). By shaking it off, they are able to release the energy or memory of the traumatic incident in their bodies. The shaking or trembling sends a signal to the animal's brain (the limbic part of the brain) to tell it to shut down the fight-or-flight response because the danger has passed. When some animals aren't able to shake off the shock, they tend to become frail and die. Human beings that cannot "shake off" the fight-or-flight response tend to develop mental and physical illnesses.

When human beings cannot shake off the trauma they've endured, it's stored in the body as a form of energy. The memory and psychological effects of the trauma get lodged in the brain and tissues of the body. This ultimately leads to a transformation of the brain and body and the person's experience of life is significantly altered. The brain and body become quite literally stuck in a survival response and are unable to restore themselves back to normal functioning. The longer the brain goes without resetting, the more likely a trauma survivor will develop PTSD.

The good news is that the human body is one of the most intelligent organisms in nature. The body wants to heal and release trapped trauma so that it can return to its natural bodily functions. There are many ways survivors can help the body naturally clear or remove the trauma energy. Below are 10 tips to release stress and heal trauma stored in the body:

1. If you find your body trembling, allow it to tremble. As mentioned above, this is a natural animal instinct to release stress. Many people notice the trembling and try to hide it or make it stop; try not to do this as it might delay the natural process of healing from shock. You'll feel a lot more relieved when it's over!
2. If you feel energy or tension in your hands, arms, or shoulders, it may be trapped from a previous "fight" response. Conversely, energy or tension in your feet or legs may be trapped from a previous "flight" response. You can release the

energy in your hands, arms, and shoulders by taking on a sport like boxing or release the energy in your feet and legs by taking part in martial arts.

3. If you suddenly feel like crying, feel free to cry. Once again, the body is processing and attempting to release a lot of stress, which includes psychological stress too. Remember to breathe while crying, getting as much oxygen as you can through your nose and out your mouth. Avoid slipping into fear-based thinking or dwelling on negative beliefs when crying.

4. Sometimes the body will experience hot and cold fever-like symptoms. Simply treat it like how you would treat normal fever symptoms and let it naturally clear on its own time.

5. If you find yourself slipping back into a state of dissociation (mentally escaping from the work of healing taking place in your body) find healthy activities to keep your mind present but also preoccupied. For instance, you can go for a walk, read a book, or practice meditation.

6. Don't be ashamed if you're sleeping a lot more. Let your body rest for as long as it wants to. Sleep is a natural technique the body uses to process and release stress. If you find that sleeping too much is making you feel lethargic, pick up a physical sport, like swimming, to revitalize your energy levels.

7. Try to reduce the amount of caffeine you consume. Caffeine can cause anxiety or stress-related side effects, which aren't helpful while your body is releasing stress. Lower your intake of caffeinated drinks like coffee, tea, or energy drinks, as well as sugar and alcohol.

8. Be more affectionate toward others and welcome the affection shown to you. A simple hug can lower stress and make you feel a lot better. Practice expressing gratitude, like saying "Thank you" or "You mean a lot to me" and enjoy the pleasurable feelings of love returned to you.

9. Remember to regulate your breathing, finding your natural rhythm, and keeping a natural pace. Take several breaks throughout the day to breathe more deeply and ease tension in your body.
10. Learn to laugh more. Laughter is medicine for the soul, it keeps you in a state of joy and makes the load on your shoulders easier to bear. Surround yourself with people that make you laugh or watch standup comedy or sitcoms you enjoy.

The EmotionAid Technique to Release Trauma from the Body

When survivors have trauma trapped in their bodies, their body immediately feels it while their minds try to make sense of it. Unfortunately, the mind cannot tell the difference between a physical and an emotional threat, thus the physiological reactions are usually just as intense when a survivor feels emotionally vulnerable as when their lives are in serious physical danger.

Once again, healing is possible and because the body is so smart, healing can occur naturally. When seeking to heal trauma in the body, the first step ought to be calming the body, switching off the fight-or-flight mode, and shifting to a more relaxed state. Gina Ross, the founder of the International Trauma-Healing Institute developed a technique known as EmotionAid, which helps in releasing trauma trapped in the body. The technique works as follows:

Step 1: Assess Your Stress Levels

Take a moment to assess your stress levels. It may help to get away from a noisy environment and sit in a quiet room where you can assess your emotional state. Rate your stress levels from one to seven: one being very low stress and seven being extreme stress. If your stress levels are really high, practice the grounding technique below to reduce the tension in your body:

- Give yourself a big hug and then alternately tap your hands on your arms. Do this 25 times and end with a deep inhale and exhale.
- In a seated position, notice the points where your body makes contact with the chair or floor. Notice your back against the chair, buttocks firmly on the seat or floor, and legs connected to the floor. Next, notice your feet pressing into the ground and sending a powerful energy force beneath to the soil. Follow this energy force as it travels, like roots, deeper and deeper into the earth. When the energy reaches the earth's core, notice it turning directions and making its way up, toward you. As it reaches your feet, notice the energy sending light through your entire body, until it reaches the crown of your head. Take several deep breaths and remain connected to the light for as long as you like.
- Place one hand on your belly and the other on your chest. Listen to the rhythm of your breathing without trying to change it. When you are ready, bring your awareness to your heartbeat and follow it without changing it.

Step 2: Discharge Sensations and Release Stress

The second step involves releasing troubling thoughts and strong emotions that have been trapped in the body. Below is an outline of the process:

- Notice your breath and any bodily sensations that you experience. When stress hormones are being released from the body, they can manifest in the form of sweating, coughing, yawning, sounds in your stomach, or changes in heart rate. When you feel these sensations, stay with them until they

naturally fade away. Avoid judging your experience or trying to make sense of it in your mind.
- Bring to mind the traumatic event that has been a constant trigger in your life. Playback the memory of what happened and notice each emotion that comes up within you. When replaying the memory, see it in slow-motion so that you can track every emotion that's triggered by the flashback.
- Feel each emotion, one at a time, and let it naturally express itself as it comes. If multiple emotions arise, select the one you wish to focus on and put the rest on an imaginary shelf. Stay with each emotion until the sensations it came with fade away.
- After addressing the emotional impact of the traumatic event, you can work through the negative thoughts you adopted as a result of the trauma. Once again, replay the memory slowly so that you can track every negative thought or belief that was created as a result of the incident. If multiple thoughts show up at the same time, select one thought to focus your attention on and put the rest on an imaginary shelf.
- Each thought will bring with it sensations, like feeling a sense of shame, disgust, humiliation, or self-judgment. Observe these sensations and the impact they have on your body. Keep observing them, without any fear, until you notice them becoming less and less existent.
- Finally, think of resources. Resources are powerful things that make you feel instantly calm and at peace. For example, a resource can be a mental picture of your spouse smiling or a fond memory of a personal achievement. Focus on one resource at a time and notice the sensations they cause you to feel. Realize that your body is able to feel, embrace, and connect with these pleasurable sensations. Stay with these sensations for as long as you like.

CHAPTER 4:

RECONNECTION AND INTEGRATION

Mikey and his family relocated to the United States after his father managed to find a job opportunity. This was great news for the family because it symbolized getting a fresh start on life again. Mikey had already learned valuable coping skills from his therapist and so his family life wasn't a source of trigger anymore for him. Nonetheless, he feared that such a dramatic move may re-traumatize him and bring back feelings of vulnerability.

None of them had traveled to the United States before, nor did they have any family living there. They were going to be the first people in their family to live in the U.S. and this brought about bitter-sweet feelings. The upside was they could be exposed to many more opportunities in the U.S., and once settled, they could help other members of their family access these opportunities too. The downside was they didn't have anyone to call when they needed assistance and didn't have a sense of community to offer support.

Only when they arrived in the United States did Mikey's father realize that his employer hadn't organized a place for them to stay. He had assumed that since he was coming from Mexico, his employer would find a temporary home for them to live in. All he had was the guarantee of a job, the rest he had to figure out on his own.

This situation had the potential to take the family on yet another downward spiral, however, they had thoroughly gone through steps one and two and had this fearless confidence when it came to overcoming obstacles. When I asked Mikey about what was going through his mind when they realized they would be homeless in another nation, he smiled and said, "We burst into a Mexican wave of laughter because we thought ' We're so screwed!'." I can almost imagine them looking at each other, with luggage on their backs, and just laughing at the absurdity of the situation they were in.

It wasn't because they thought it was funny, but because they understood that they had no control over their circumstance and had to make lemonade out of lemons. The family lived on the streets of Houston for several months before moving to a house in a Hispanic community. Mikey says that the time on the streets felt shorter than it actually was because his family had come to terms with their life situation. They weren't fighting the natural progression of life anymore, but instead went along with whichever direction they were being pulled in.

They were comfortable in who they were, so much that life circumstances weren't triggering to them. Of course, they still felt disappointed and frustrated with the pace at which life was moving, however, they weren't fearful of what would happen to them or whether they would survive the next obstacle. Stage three in the healing and recovery process from trauma is all about reconnecting to the person you are and reintegrating yourself into society, letting go of the fears that were brought about by the painful event or period in your life. Mikey had reached stage four and he had so many valuable lessons to share with me about the joys of reconnecting to his body and redesigning his new life post-trauma

Being Comfortable in Your Own Skin

Mikey was a confident young man and it showed in how he spoke and in how warm he was with other people. When I asked him about how he cultivated his level of confidence, he took me back to when he started working in Houston. He found a job at a nearby restaurant and worked as a waiter. He didn't particularly like his job because it had him on his feet most of the day, and he preferred sketching designs in his graphic design software. Nevertheless, he appreciated his job because it allowed him to contribute to the household income. His father didn't need any help at that particular point but Mikey still felt obligated.

Mikey said that one day, while working a night shift, a group of White Texan boys walked into the restaurant, demanding to be served. He could hear them from across the room and decided to attend to them so that they wouldn't disturb the other customers. Little did he know that by serving them, he'd experience a xenophobic attack. It started "playful," with some of the boys asking him where he was from and what life was like in Mexico. It then became offensive when the boys mumbled Spanish phrases that didn't sound correct or make any sense. When he asked them to stop, they told him that he was on their territory now (referencing America) and that he was powerless over them.

Walking back to the kitchen, Mikey took a moment to recollect himself and think of the best way to interpret the situation he was in. He had a few options, either:

- He could interpret the situation as a personal attack on his identity;
- He could interpret the situation as an attack on his family's traumatic past;
- He could interpret the situation as a sign of being rejected in this new country;

- He could interpret the situation as ignorance by uneducated boys.

He chose to go with the last one, deciding not to reopen wounds from his past. He saw the behavior of the boys as foolish and embarrassing considering how old they were. Yes, he was offended by the xenophobic attacks but he was secure enough in himself to not let their racist sentiments define who he was. Instead, he thought it would be funny to play a prank on them since they were so childish. He told the chefs to put their food on the side because he wanted to plate them up a hearty starter.

He went outside with two plates and piled a lot of soil and dirt on each plate. He did this with another two plates as well. On the kitchen table were four plates full of soil and dirt, ready to be served to the boys. As he put the plates before the boys, their eyes shot up at Mikey, wondering what kind of game he was playing. Mikey cleared his throat and said, "Gentlemen, please enjoy a starter of freshly watered American soil. This one is on the house."

When I heard the story, I couldn't stop myself from laughing. Mikey had good stories, but this one took the cake. I wish I was there to see the confusion on their faces. The story taught me a valuable lesson about confidence. I learned that true confidence isn't tied to what others do or how others react, rather, it was about how you chose to look at yourself and respond to whatever life throws at you. Below are a few more tips I've collected over the years on how to be comfortable in your own skin:

Tip 1: Take Care of Yourself

Regularly check-in on your mental and emotional state. It can be as simple as stopping whatever you're doing, taking a few deep breaths, and asking yourself "How are you doing?" There are so many triggering moments that occur throughout the day, but it doesn't mean you need to be triggered by them. Practice listing all of the options you have in how you want to perceive the situation and choose one that supports your own health.

Tip 2: Feed Your Mind

Knowledge is power and it's also extremely liberating! Learn about your emotional triggers, or the various ways your trauma can manifest in your life. This will help you feel more in control when you are triggered because you understand why and how the trigger came to be. Watch videos of how other people who survived a similar trauma coped after experiencing trauma and listen to music or podcasts that uplifts your soul.

Tip 3: Be Curious About Yourself

Enjoy the journey of finding yourself! It's an incredible journey that only you can travel. Find out the complexities of your personality and some of your quirks that make you special. If you have a talent, look into it and find out how deep it goes. Challenge yourself about some of your beliefs and play "What if" scenarios to see how you would respond to various situations.

Tip 4: Stop Caring What Other People Think

The quickest way to reduce your self-esteem is to think about the horrible or judgmental things that other people may or may not be saying about you. Honestly speaking, how much of your life do they even know to be able to form concrete opinions about who you are? Focus your energy on the steps you're taking to rebuild yourself and cultivate happiness in your life.

Tip 5: Realize That You Don't Have to Do Anything

How many times do you pretend to like something only because other people like it? Or agree to plans because you don't want to make the organizer upset? Part of being comfortable with who you are involves honoring how you feel and only doing things that make you feel good about yourself. You don't have to feel pressured to do anything that makes you go against your own values.

Tip 6: It's Okay to Say No

Saying "No" to people doesn't make you a bad or selfish person. In fact, when you say "No" to things that don't honor who you are, you're actually saying "Yes" to yourself! Before committing to any plans or making any decisions, ask yourself if you really want to make the commitment or not. You're not obligated to make other people happy at your own expense.

Building Trust in Relationships Post-Trauma

Mikey's family was tight-knit, but I wondered how he was able to rebuild trust in his friendships or romantic relationships post-trauma. He told me that the toughest part about learning to love someone else after experiencing trauma is fearing that the other person might trigger those old emotional wounds. He knew what it felt like to lose control over his mind and body, and he was afraid that by letting someone in and opening up to them, he might just lose touch with who he was.

However, he loved himself enough to know that he deserved to be loved by another person and to offer love in return. From his new friends, he craved the kind of brotherhood he had with his friends growing up, and from a partner, he desired to be nurtured and supported in his dreams.

Mikey only had one condition which he wouldn't compromise on. He needed to have relationships that felt safe and allowed him to freely express himself. He refused to be surrounded by people with whom he couldn't have real and meaningful discussions. He had been to rock bottom alone, and he didn't want to feel lonely in his suffering ever again. 'The trick to healthy relationships after trauma," Mikey said, "is to cultivate an environment that continually offers healing." I was curious what this kind of environment would look like, so he gave me few pointers:

Take Responsibility for How You Feel (and Vice Versa)

Mikey told me that in order to build respect in relationships, all parties involved needed to take responsibility for their own feelings and avoid pushing them on others. It's not the other person's responsibility to make you happy or inspire you; you are the only one who holds the keys to your happiness.

Assume the Best of Each Other

When a friend or partner does something to hurt you, assume that they did it unintentionally. Always see them as being on your team and helping you be the best version of yourself that you can be. When you assume the worst in a person, you begin to feed yourself negative thoughts, which end up creating trouble in healthy relationships. Give your loved ones the benefit of the doubt; they're human too!

Think Before You Speak

Sometimes when we're triggered, we can speak impulsively which causes our loved ones a lot of pain. It's better to take a moment and process the strong emotions you're feeling before continuing on the discussion or argument. Choose to respond with words that can bring resolve and peace to the relationship. If you cannot express yourself verbally, put your thoughts and feelings in writing.

Leave Your Expectations at the Door

Expectations lead to disappointment. It's impossible to assume that our friends and family will behave according to our standards, principles, or values. Love is meant to be unconditional, which means we love and accept others as they are. It's better to take people at face value than to fantasize about who they are and how they can treat you.

Be Quick to Move On

When your loved ones offend you, don't hold onto the grudge. Be quick to forgive and remember that it's natural for people to offend you. Nobody is perfect and it's unfair to expect people to act perfectly. First, find ways of resolving the matter. Then, make sure the wrongdoer will commit to their promise to be considerate of your boundaries and emotions.

Setting Meaningful Personal and Professional Goals

Mikey was motivated to make something of his life. He didn't want to live in the shadows of his past trauma forever. Since he loved drawing, he decided to go back to school and study to become a graphic designer. His degree opened so many doors for him, like working at the marketing agency I had met him at. According to him, having a sense of purpose helped in his healing journey. It gave him something different to preoccupy his mind with and goals to reach for.

Finding a sense of purpose isn't easy. It requires you to first be comfortable in your own skin and then to search your heart to find your deepest desires. Mikey's deepest desire was to create art that could inspire others. That led him into the graphic design field, however, it could also lead him down many other paths in the future.

While setting meaningful goals can be a positive step in recovery, it can also become a source of stress for those who are living with PTSD. For example, if the goal seems too lofty or far-fetched, it can cause a sufferer to feel anxious about reaching their goal or lead to procrastination. The last thing anyone wants is to be discouraged by something that's supposed to empower them. Below are a few tips on how to set personal and professional goals without letting them overwhelm you:

Tip 1: Break Down Your Goals into Smaller Ones

When a goal is too big, you are more likely to be discouraged while pursuing it. Breaking goals into smaller, achievable pieces can help you complete tasks quicker and with more confidence. Celebrate each small victory and let the momentum of your victory push you toward achieving the next small goal.

Tip 2: Think About Your WHY

Whenever you pursue a goal it's important to consider the intention behind it. Ask yourself what this goal means to you and why you feel a strong need to achieve it. Strong intentions are able to keep you focused on your goal and resilient through tough times.

Tip 3: Encourage Yourself with Positive Self-Talk

When it comes to setting and pursuing goals, you need to become your own cheerleader. When you're feeling low, you can find positive affirmations to say to yourself; and when you succeed, you can find ways to reward yourself for all of your hard work. Remember, self-compassion is more useful than self-criticism.

Tip 4: Be Flexible Enough to Make Adjustments

Life is unpredictable. There are so many unforeseen events that occur without any warning. These unforeseen events can delay your plans or completely ruin them. Be flexible enough to make adjustments when these unexpected events occur. For example, if your plans to go back to school have been delayed due to Covid-19, you can find other ways to study online or at least get a headstart in the field you're hoping to get into.

Tip 5: There's No Such Thing as Perfection

Don't beat yourself up about the time it takes to achieve your goals or how meticulous you want your plans to be. When your standards are too high, you're more likely to be disappointed when your plans look or feel different than what you expected. Learn to embrace your mistakes and find the lesson behind each one.

CHAPTER 5:

POST-TRAUMATIC GROWTH (PTG)

Through talking with Mikey, I found that there are survivors who are able to find the purpose in their pain. Through understanding their experience, they are able to regain control in their lives and reclaim their identity. Of course, recovering from trauma is an emotionally taxing process, but these survivors are willing to confront their pain and overcome it.

Not many people reach stage three, and even fewer will get to stage four. Stage four is the post-traumatic growth (PTG) stage and it describes the kind of positive transformation some trauma survivors experience as part of their recovery. Have you ever met someone who had gone through the worst kind of tragedy but was able to bounce back and experience profound peace and self-actualization in their lives? Mikey fit this box for me. If you didn't know his history, you'd think he grew up in a stable environment and received all of the emotional and physical nurturing he needed. Mikey's happiness went deeper than his smile or his unforgettable laugh; that man's happiness was rooted from within. Below are some of the truths that helped Mikey experience growth post-trauma.

Self-Awareness Leads to Happiness

Self-awareness is the ability to have a sober perception of your personality, talents, strengths, weaknesses, and beliefs. A person with high levels of self-awareness can trace every feeling they're experiencing to a recent thought or behavior. They understand themselves so well that it brings about a strong feeling of self-love and self-acceptance. By understanding themselves, they're also able to understand other people's behaviors and the attitudes that people have toward them.

Self-awareness can help you achieve your dreams. When you know who you are and what you're capable of, you're more likely to see opportunities in the skills, resources, and personality traits you already have. This helps you focus on your strengths and what you have access to, to move you closer and closer to your dreams. Self-awareness also helps you regulate your ego and other negative thoughts or emotions that aren't helpful for your personal growth. You can easily detect when your self-talk is negative and investigate where these negative suggestions come from.

Below are 10 questions that you can ask yourself to assess how self-aware you are:

1. How would you describe yourself in three words?
2. What's the one thing you desire in life?
3. What role have you played in creating your current life situation?
4. What makes you feel afraid?
5. What quality do you think is unique about you?
6. What quality do you value in other people?
7. How do you cope with stress?
8. How do you manage your emotions?
9. If you had to change one thing about yourself, what would you change?

10. What are some values you won't compromise on in relationships?

Self-awareness leads to happiness because you're able to find solutions to your inner discomfort and immediately respond to your needs. For example, after he left school, Mikey worked at a nearby restaurant. He had enough self-awareness to realize that:

- He wasn't happy at his job.
- He saw himself working in another industry, such as the creative arts.
- He couldn't quit because he felt the need to help his family financially.
- He was able to cope with the demands of his current job because helping his family financially was something he deeply valued.

Through practicing self-awareness, Mikey was able to find happiness at his job, even though it wasn't his ideal career. What made him happy at work wasn't the environment, but the fact that his monthly salary could help his family with household expenses. Since helping out his family was something he deeply valued, working at the restaurant wasn't as torturous as it could've been. Below are a few tips on how you can grow in self-awareness and take a hold of your happiness too:

Tip 1: Look at Yourself Objectively

Part of becoming self-aware requires you to separate yourself from your emotional experience. Sometimes, your emotional experience can cloud what's actually happening around you or what you truly think matters. Practice being the observer or third-party that looks at your life from an outside-in perspective. As the observer, you don't have any biases toward what's happening, you're simply looking and interpreting what you see. Write down the observations you have about your current life situation and notice how differently these observations look without any emotional influence.

Tip 2: Journal Your Thoughts

Writing can be a form of therapy, helping you express what you're feeling on paper. By journaling your thoughts, you'll be able to track what you think about most, what scares you, or what brings you fulfillment. There's so much you can learn about yourself by simply reading some of the notes you've made in your journal.

Tip 3: Don't Judge How You Feel

On your road to recovery, you want to feel good every day, although healing isn't a linear process. There will be days when you slip back into old thinking patterns or feel stuck in a rut. Don't judge how you feel on those days. Instead, figure out what caused you to adopt old beliefs about yourself or your life and confront it head on. It's also important to remember that there isn't a particular feeling that's prohibited for you to feel (you can learn as much from anger as you can from peace).

Resilience in the Face of Adversity

When Richard Tedeschi and Lawrence Calhoun came up with the term "Post-traumatic growth" they defined it as being positive psychological change a survivor would experience after overcoming an extremely challenging situation. One of the major themes of post-traumatic growth is resilience - being able to withstand and persevere through hard times.

There are four types of resilience: physical, mental, emotional, and social.

Physical resilience describes the body's ability to withstand physical strain and recover quickly when it's injured. Physical resilience can help you commit to fitness goals such as losing weight or help you cope after undergoing invasive surgery. Mental resilience refers to the ability of the mind to absorb and retain information, problem solve, consider alternatives, and come up with effective strategies on how to reach your goals.

Emotional resilience is closely related to emotional intelligence and refers to the ability to accept your current life situation, persevere through hardship, and be optimistic about the future. Emotional resilience can help you make the necessary adjustments to your life after a sudden change, and to think positively when situations look discouraging. Social resilience refers to the ability to connect with others socially; it must be built on a foundation of mutual respect, trust, and acceptance. Social resilience is seen in how communities come together to offer support in times of crisis or simply make an effort to smile at others, greet with a firm handshake, and get to know people through meaningful conversations.

Below are three steps to cultivating your personal strength and learning how to be more resilient during tough times:

Step 1: Reframe Your Perceptions

Resilient people have a very unique way of describing their personal experiences to themselves. They are careful not to describe their experience negatively, otherwise, they might become discouraged and retreat. Instead, they learn how to frame their experience in a way that empowers them to be grateful for where they currently are. For example, when a resilient person cannot find a job regardless of how hard they try, they see their unemployment as being a time to refine their skills and engage in activities that would later make their resume look more attractive. A resilient person never sees themselves as getting the shorter end of the stick; in their eyes, every situation is helping them reach their dreams.

Step 2: Identify What Is Within Your Control

Resilient people don't stress about factors out of their control. They know that their strength is limited (self-awareness) and that they can only do a finite amount of things to improve their health, career, or relationships. For example, a resilient person knows that they can control the quality of food they eat and how much exercise they do, but they cannot control contracting an illness. Likewise, they know that they can control how they treat people but cannot control how others behave toward them. Identifying what you can control is liberating because it means you can let go of trying to solve issues that you can't do anything about.

Step 3: Embrace Your Failures

Failure is an integral part of success. It's impossible to accomplish anything in life without having been through a few obstacles to get there. Therefore, failure shouldn't be something that we run away from, it should be something we embrace. Instead of seeing failure as an opportunity to quit, see it as an opportunity to learn. What can your failures teach you about planning ahead? Managing your time efficiently? Communicating with others? Or seeking assistance when you need it? Find out what you can learn from every setback so that you can rise even stronger than you were before.

CHAPTER 6:

MIND-BODY APPROACHES FOR EMOTIONAL TRAUMA PROCESSING

Since the body is where trauma resides, it's so important to learn techniques of how to process and release trauma from the body. The only way to heal is to feel and confront the heaviness that was left in your body after a traumatic experience. Below are two approaches you can take to help you accept, process, and release trauma from your body:

Acceptance and Commitment Therapy

Acceptance and commitment therapy (ACT) encourages people to freely engage with their thoughts and emotions rather than hiding them or denying that they exist. ACT combines mindfulness skills with practices of self-acceptance in order to face a problem and overcome it.

A therapist helps you work through your own self-talk and how you perceive your life situation, traumatic events that have occurred, dysfunctional relationships, or any physical limitations you may have. You are then given an opportunity to decide whether a particular issue requires immediate action or whether it can be accepted for what it is while you work on making necessary behavioral changes that could change the outcome of the situation later.

A key focus in ACT is developing personal values (what you stand for) and setting meaningful goals to help you achieve your desired life. However, the biggest threat to your future is fear. Fear can stand in your way and can cause you to resort back to old ways of thinking and interpreting your life. An ACTs exercise, part of The Happiness Trap looks at overcoming F.E.A.R., an acronym used to describe the common barriers standing in your path of healing and growth:

F = Fusion (the negative suggestions your mind gives you when you're trying to make positive progress)

E = Excessive goals (goals that are too big or require skills that you don't yet have)

A = Avoidance of discomfort (Getting out of your comfort zone and being afraid of the challenges you might face)

R = Remoteness from values (Losing touch with what's important to you)

The exercise requires you to write a list of all the things that have come in the way of you pursuing your goals. After creating this list, go back and label each answer with one of the F.E.A.R. letters (whichever letter best describes the barrier). For example, if you have been hindered by negative beliefs about your own capabilities, you would label those with an "F." If you lacked resources, like time or money, you would label those barriers with an "E."

The solution for removing F.E.A.R. is to D.A.R.E. In essence, D.A.R.E. provides the reversal of all the barriers that caused you not to take any action. The acronym stands for:

D = Defusion

A = Acceptance of discomfort

R = Realistic goals

E = Embracing values

Refer back to your list of barriers and work through each barrier, finding ways to reverse them to embrace D.A.R.E. For example, you could challenge your negative beliefs and create positive affirmations to counter the inner self-critic. You could also break down your goals into smaller ones, starting with those you can financially afford to implement.

Mindfulness Meditation

Another great approach for working through trauma is by practicing mindfulness meditation. Mindfulness helps to slow down the movement of the mind and bring your attention to the present moment. It also gives you an opportunity to see or experience your inner discomfort, staying with it until it dissolves into nothing. This may be triggering for some survivors, especially if they aren't yet ready to confront their strong emotions.

The essence of mindfulness is to gather your mind into the here and now. This helps to calm your mind and free it from heavy thoughts about the past or anxieties about the future. It also frees you emotionally as you realize how much power and control you have in the here and now, as compared to the hopelessness you felt in the past and the lack of control you have about the future.

Over time, practicing mindfulness meditation can reduce the intensity and frequency of PTSD symptoms and help you reconnect with your mind and body. It can help you develop a sense of safety in your current life situation and feel grounded in who you are. Practicing mindfulness also has positive physiological effects on your body, such as improving your ability to focus on tasks, reducing your levels of stress or anxiety, and releasing muscle tension and body aches.

Below is a mindfulness meditation script to help you let go of heavy thoughts in your mind:

I invite you to sit in a comfortable position, either on a chair or on the floor. You can use the back of the chair to support your back, otherwise, ensure that your back is straight. Rest your arms on your legs and allow your shoulders to recline naturally. Pay attention to your breathing; notice the rhythm and speed of your breath.

When you are ready, you will send a sense of calm throughout your body by following a breathing technique. You will inhale deeply for five counts, pause for one count, and then exhale slowly for another five counts. Repeat this breathing exercise until your body is completely relaxed.

When you notice thoughts arising in your head, witness them without opening or digging deeper into them. See them as clouds that float into your mind and gradually float away. You cannot grasp a cloud; you can only observe its unique shape or marvel at its beauty. Avoid chasing after these clouds. Remain grounded in your breathing.

Allow your thoughts to come and go as they please. There are no thoughts that are more highly favored than the rest. Feel a sense of love for the thoughts that come in and out of your mind. Since you cannot change them, connect with them through love. Avoid being swept away in your expression of love; remain grounded in your breathing.

Remember that you are not your thoughts, but only the one who has the privilege of witnessing them. Feel a sense of gratitude for having such varied, complex, and intriguing thoughts.

Focus your attention back on your breathing. Feel empowered by every inhale and exhale breath. At this moment, you are in control. Imagine that with each breath, you are getting stronger, wiser, and more resilient. When you are ready you can continue with the rest of your day.

A LETTER TO MY SPECIAL READER

Dear Reader,

I thank you for having the courage to pick up this book. You may have experienced trauma in your life or know of someone close to you who has experienced trauma. This book has offered you a key to unlock yourself from the prison of your mind. It has shown you that healing is possible if that is truly what you desire.

There is no amount of emotional pain that is incurable. Your human body was built to naturally heal itself from emotional trauma. Don't you feel your heart protesting for peace? Or your chest burning for you to finally take a stand and declare your freedom? I want to encourage you that your mind and body are on your side, cheering you on with their subtle whispers. We want you to recover and feel alive again! It may take you many months to get through each stage of healing and I want you to know that's normal.

Fortunately, there are no time frames concerning when you are expected to feel better or take decisions to improve your life. As long as you're still mentally committed to your journey, you're a winner in my eyes.

Remember to be gentle with yourself; self-compassion is far more empowering than self-criticism. Eventually, you will learn to love the person you see in the mirror, but for now, keep speaking positive words to yourself and feeding your mind with sound wisdom.

Healing is a journey and there will be many times where you feel it's too hard to carry on. The journey can be rough, however, it's so worth it and you will thank yourself once you have reached the other side. You deserve to put yourself first and prioritize your well-being.

I wish you the very best,

Allison.

CONCLUSION

Emotional trauma isn't easy to process. It leaves open wounds, which have the potential to change who you are when they aren't attended to. Confronting these wounds isn't easy or pleasurable. Who really wants to relive horrific memories from their past? It's far easier to pretend as though these wounds don't exist and that they don't have any effect on normal daily life. However, your past trauma can also be used as a tool to spear-head you into a healthier and prosperous future. Unchaining your trauma can be a liberating experience, offering you insight into the lessons that can be learned from the past.

I imagine this is what Macy ended up doing. After a few months or years, she realized that there was so much life to live and experience and that her thoughts and unresolved emotions were keeping her in chains. I always knew her as a fighter and I have no doubt she fought for her peace and finally reconnected to who she was.

The only way out is through. Freedom from the past comes when we finally decide to confront our past and close that chapter of our lives. The past is only relevant for as long as we make it. I understand how difficult it must have been for a survivor like Macy to come to terms with some of the horrific events that had occurred in her life, and like many survivors, reclaiming her sense of freedom was a journey.

It's possible for a survivor to regress in their healing journey because they are human and each of us process pain differently. It's okay to have a bad day or to forget all of the healing steps. It doesn't cancel or nullify all of the amazing progress you have made so far. It's just a bump on the road which you can recover from, so don't shame yourself for it or let it weigh you down—acknowledge it, feel it, and push through.

The manner in which Mikey dealt with his family's financial woes and homelessness left took me by surprise. I couldn't believe how resilient someone could be after having experienced some of the worst life experiences. Mikey knew early on that dissociating from his current life experiences meant that he would be disconnected from his mind and body. He wouldn't be able to connect with those he loved or even connect with his own needs and his passion for drawing.

He faced his pain and accepted his life circumstance for what it was. This brought about a sense of freedom amidst the turmoil. He was no longer tied to his tragedy, nor did he allow it to define him. For this, I applaud him.

While emotional trauma isn't easy to process, you owe it to yourself to find ways of addressing so you can live the kind of life you hope for. Remember that you are not defined by what happened to you. You are powerful and worthy of an incredible and satisfying life. You can chain your trauma and leave it in the past where it belongs and focus on the next moves you desire to take in your life. I am rooting for you!

Chain Your Trauma – Train Your Change

REFERENCES

Addiction Prevention Coalition. (2019, October 1). *Denial: Why it happens and how to overcome it*. APCBham. https://apcbham.org/2019/10/01/denial-why-it-happens-and-how-to-overcome-it/

Amber and the Team. (2020, December 2). *How to feel comfortable in your own skin*. Https://Www.shinesheets.com/. https://www.shinesheets.com/how-to-be-more-comfortable-in-your-own-skin/

Andersen, N. (2017, December 17). *Types of resilience*. Open Pages. https://openpagesweb.wordpress.com/2017/12/17/types-of-resilience/

Axelrod, J. (2016, May 17). *How Does PTSD Affect Relationships?* Psych Central. https://psychcentral.com/lib/ptsd-and-relationships

Byock, S. D. (2016, November 11). *20 Tips to release stress and heal trauma*. Satya Doyle Byock, LPC. https://quarterlife.org/blog/2016/11/11/20-tips-to-release-stress-and-heal-trauma-from-this-election

Cafasso, J. (2017, July 8). *Traumatic events: Causes, effects, and management*. Healthline. https://www.healthline.com/health/traumatic-events#responses-to-trauma

Carpenter, D. (2020, March 6). *How to enhance your resilience to bounce back after tough times*. Verywell Mind. https://www.verywellmind.com/how-to-build-resilience-for-tough-times-1717568

Chen, L. (2015, October 19). *7 Things your inner child needs to hear you say*. Tiny Buddha. https://tinybuddha.com/blog/7-things-your-inner-child-needs-to-hear-you-say/

Collier, L. (2016, November). Growth after trauma. *Https://Www.apa.org*. https://www.apa.org/monitor/2016/11/growth-trauma

Drillinger, M. (2018, August 21). *6 Things I learned from dating someone with PTSD*. Healthline. https://www.healthline.com/health/mental-health/lessons-partner-with-ptsd#6.-Its-OK-to-walk-away

Foy, C. (2019, August 29). *Why people with PTSD withdrawal: Stuck in a cycle of isolation*. FHE Health – Addiction & Mental Health Care. https://fherehab.com/learning/reasons-ptsd-self-isolating/

Fredrek, C. (2018, September 4). *3 Stages of recovery from trauma & PTSD in therapy*. Healing Matters. https://healingmatters.ca/3-stages-of-recovery-from-trauma-ptsd-in-therapy/

Goldstein, E. (n.d.). *Learning to love after trauma — Integrative psychotherapy and trauma treatment*. Integrative Psychotherapy & Trauma Treatment. Retrieved February 19, 2021, from https://integrativepsych.co/new-blog/relationship-counseling-5towns-nassau-long-island

Harris, R. (2008). *Worksheets to use with The Happiness Trap*. http://thehappinesstrap.com/upimages/The_Complete_Happiness_Trap_Worksheets.pdf.pdf

High Focus Centers. (2020, May 18). *3 Pillars for creating a safe space: Managing trauma symptoms during COVID-19*. High Focus

Centers. https://highfocuscenters.pyramidhealthcarepa.com/the-3-pillars-for-creating-a-safe-space-managing-trauma-symptoms-during-covid-19/

Jacobson. (2017, March 23). *What is the "Inner Child"?* Harley Therapy™ Blog. https://www.harleytherapy.co.uk/counselling/what-is-the-inner-child.htm

Kee, A. (2016, August 29). *The denial of trauma.* Psych Central. https://psychcentral.com/blog/the-denial-of-trauma#3

Keely. (2019, October 14). *How to cultivate strong self awareness for your happiness and health.* Creating Sunflowers. https://creatingsunflowers.com/blog/2019/10/14/how-to-cultivate-strong-self-awareness-for-your-happiness-and-health

Kelloway, R. (2020, July 27). *How to release trauma trapped in the body.* Life Care Wellness. https://life-care-wellness.com/how-to-release-trauma-trapped-in-the-body/

Linder, J. N. (2019, September 19). *What is trauma, and can mindfulness help treat it?* Psychology Today. https://www.psychologytoday.com/us/blog/mindfulness-insights/201909/what-is-trauma-and-can-mindfulness-help-treat-it

Luna, A. (2019, April 6). *25 Signs you have a wounded inner child (and how to heal).* LonerWolf. https://lonerwolf.com/feeling-safe-inner-child/

McAllister, J. (2017, August 18). *Resensitization: Coming back to life after trauma.* GoodTherapy.org Therapy Blog. https://www.goodtherapy.org/blog/resensitization-coming-back-to-life-after-trauma-0223154

Millan, K. (n.d.). *Signs and symptoms of PTSD*. Black Bear Lodge. Retrieved February 12, 2021, from https://blackbearrehab.com/mental-health/ptsd/signs-and-symptoms-of-ptsd/

Peterson, S. (2018, November 5). *About child trauma*. The National Child Traumatic Stress Network. https://www.nctsn.org/what-is-child-trauma/about-child-trauma

Scott, S. J. (2019, January 12). *How to be more self aware: 8 Tips to boost self-awareness*. Develop Good Habits. https://www.developgoodhabits.com/what-is-self-awareness/

Shaw, B. (2019, October 23). *When trauma gets stuck in the body*. Psychology Today. https://www.psychologytoday.com/us/blog/in-the-body/201910/when-trauma-gets-stuck-in-the-body

Swan, T. (n.d.). *Denial (and how to get out of denial)*. Teal Swan. Retrieved February 16, 2021, from https://tealswan.com/resources/articles/denial-and-how-to-get-out-of-denial-r236/

Tull, M. (2019, June 3). *The double-edged sword of childhood trauma and dissociation*. Verywell Mind. https://www.verywellmind.com/how-trauma-can-lead-to-dissociative-disorders-2797534

Tull, M. (2020, February 12). *Why people with PTSD should learn how to set and manage goals*. Verywell Mind. https://www.verywellmind.com/setting-and-managing-goals-

2797566

U.S. Department of Veterans Affairs. (2020, January 14). *Relationships - PTSD: National Center for PTSD*. Www.ptsd.va.gov. https://www.ptsd.va.gov/family/effect_relationships.asp

Made in the USA
Middletown, DE
11 October 2021